A Guide for Using

My Brother Sam Is Dead

in the Classroom

Based on the novel written by
James Lincoln Collier and Christopher Collier

This guide written by **Corinne Coombs**

Teacher Created Materials, Inc.
6421 Industry Way
Westminster, CA 92683
www.teachercreated.com
©*1999 Teacher Created Materials, Inc.*
Reprinted, 2003
Made in U.S.A.
ISBN-1-57690-507-1

Edited by
Dona Herweck Rice

Illustrated by
Howard Chaney

Cover Art by
Wendy Chang

Table of Contents

Introduction

A good book can touch our lives like a good friend. Within its pages are words and characters that can inspire us to achieve our highest ideals. We can turn to it for companionship, recreation, comfort, and guidance. It also gives us a cherished story to hold in our hearts forever.

In Literature Units, great care has been taken to select books that are sure to become good friends!

Teachers who use this unit will find the following features to supplement their own valuable ideas.

- Sample Lesson Plan
- Pre-reading Activities
- A Biographical Sketch and Picture of the Authors
- A Book Summary
- Vocabulary Lists and Vocabulary Activities
- Chapters grouped for study, with each section including

    —a quiz

    —a hands-on project

    —a cooperative learning activity

    —a cross-curriculum connection

    —an extension into the reader's own life

- Post-reading Activities
- Book Report Ideas
- Research Ideas
- A Culminating Activity
- Three Options for Unit Tests
- A Bibliography of Related Reading
- An Answer Key

We are confident that this unit will be a valuable addition to your planning, and we hope that as you use our ideas, your students will increase the circle of friends they have in books.

Sample Lesson Plan

Lesson 1
- Introduce and complete some or all of the pre-reading activities on page 5.
- Read About the Authors with your students (page 6).
- Introduce the vocabulary list for Section 1 (page 8).
- Ask students to find possible definitions for these words.

Lesson 2
- Read Chapters 1–3. As you read, place the vocabulary words in the context of the story and discuss their meanings.
- Choose a vocabulary activity (page 9).
- Dress Tim in Revolutionary War-era clothing (page 11).
- Debate the positions of Patriots and Tories (page 12).
- Complete the Revolutionary War Time Line (page 13).
- Discuss whether students would favor their fathers or brothers (page 14).
- Administer the Section 1 quiz (page 10).
- Introduce the vocabulary list for Section 2 (page 8).
- Ask students to find definitions for these words.

Lesson 3
- Read Chapters 4–6. Place the vocabulary words in context and discuss their meanings.
- Choose a vocabulary activity (page 9).
- Write lyrics to "Yankee Doodle Dandy" and sing them in class (page 16).
- Write the second letter to Mr. Burr (page 17).
- Discuss the right to bear arms (page 18).
- Discuss lying to parents and the consequences (page 19).
- Administer the Section 2 quiz (page 15).
- Introduce the vocabulary lists for Section 3 (page 8).

Lesson 4
- Read Chapters 7–9. Place the vocabulary words in context and discuss their meanings.
- Select a vocabulary activity (page 9).
- Pack for a journey (page 21).
- Map and illustrate Tim's trip to Verplancks Point and write a journal entry for Tim (page 22).
- Discuss the shortage of supplies and why there is a shortage during the war (page 23).

- Explore the meaning of sin in Tim's life and the students' reactions to Tim's thoughts and actions (page 24).
- Administer the Section 3 quiz (page 20).
- Introduce the vocabulary list for Section 4 (page 8).
- Ask students to find definitions for these words.

Lesson 5
- Read Chapters 10–12. Place the vocabulary words in context and discuss their meanings.
- Choose a vocabulary activity (page 9).
- Make a Revolutionary War flag (page 26).
- Discuss what will happen to Sam in the future (page 27).
- Investigate the death of Crispus Attucks and write a letter to the British about Ned (page 28).
- Write a letter to General Parsons to help Sam (page 29).
- Administer the Section 4 quiz (page 25).
- Introduce the vocabulary list for Section 5 (page 8).
- Ask students to find definitions for these words.

Lesson 6
- Read Chapters 13 through the epilogue.
- Choose a vocabulary activity (page 9).
- Make a map of the major battles of the Revolutionary War (page 31).
- Conduct a scavenger hunt on the Internet to find out about famous Americans (page 32).
- Create a graph of the casualties in some battles of the war (pages 33 and 34).
- Write Sam's eulogy (page 35).
- Administer the Section 5 quiz (page 30).

Lesson 7
- Assign book report and research projects (pages 36 and 37).
- Begin work on the culminating activity (pages 38 through 41).

Lesson 8
- Administer unit tests 1, 2, and/or 3 (pages 42, 43, and 44).
- Discuss the unit test answers and possibilities.
- Discuss the students' enjoyment of the book.
- Provide a list of related reading for your students (page 45).
- Complete the culminating activity (pages 38–41).

Before the Book

Before you begin reading *My Brother Sam Is Dead* with your students, do some pre-reading activities to stimulate interest and enhance comprehension. Here are some activities that might work well in your class.

1. Predict what the story might be about by hearing the title.

2. Predict what the story might be about by looking at the cover illustration.

3. Discuss other books about soldiers and war that students may have heard about or read.

4. Discuss the causes of the Revolutionary War.

5. Discuss the dissension among the colonists regarding the need for war and loyalty to the king.

6. Study the geography of the colonies, specifically the northeastern colonies.

7. Answer these questions:

   • What do you know about the American Revolution?

   • Are you interested in books concerning the relationships among family members?

   • Are you interested in stories about young people proving themselves?

   • Do you enjoy books with battles, spies, and adventures?

   • Would you ever disobey your parents to fight in a war?

   • Would you ever fight in a war in which you might kill friends and relatives?

   • Would you ever try to help someone escape from jail?

8. Discuss what it would have been like to live during the Revolutionary War and colonial America.

9. Discuss any national current events that have created dissension among citizens.

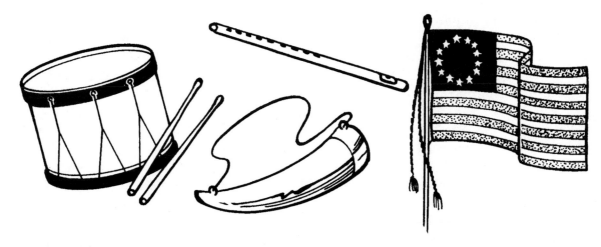

About the Authors

James Lincoln Collier was born on June 27, 1928, in New York, New York, and his brother, Christopher Collier, was born two years later on January 29, 1930. The boys were born into a family of writers and worked most of their lives as educators and authors. Christopher Collier says the reason his family writes for a living is because an author can be flexible with his time. An author does not have a set schedule, and he can work in his own way and pace.

James Lincoln Collier was an established children's author before he and his brother wrote *My Brother Sam Is Dead*. His works were based on a variety of topics, but he wrote a great deal for children about his love of jazz music. He says that he became a writer because it was the family business, and it never occurred to him that he could not write.

Christopher Collier

James Lincoln Collier

Christopher Collier is a professor of history. He wrote a variety of materials for adults before he approached his brother to collaborate on writing a historical novel for young adults. The younger Collier would do all the historical research for the books while the older brother would write the plots and characters for the story. Christopher expends a substantial amount of time and energy on research to be sure his books are as factual as possible. He even checks the weather reports of the days that are mentioned in the books to be sure that the weather described in the novel is the same as that which really occurred on that day.

My Brother Sam Is Dead is the first novel that the two brothers have written together. The book has been highly praised, and the two have gone on to write more novels from the same time period as well as other times in history. James Lincoln and Christopher Collier have enjoyed writing novels for young adults because they feel that reading the novels can make the study of history both enjoyable and exciting.

My Brother Sam Is Dead

by James Lincoln Collier and Christopher Collier

(Scholastic, 1974)

(Available from Scholastic, Canada; Scholastic Limited, UK; Prentice Hall, AUS)

My Brother Sam Is Dead tells the story of the Revolutionary War from the perspective of Tim Meeker, an adolescent boy and the younger of two sons in a Loyalist family. The story begins when Tim's brother, Sam, comes home from college dressed in a Patriot uniform and informs his family about the Patriot victory at Lexington. Tim's family, along with many of the families in Redding, Connecticut, staunchly supports the British king, and they are not in favor of the rebellion. Tim's father, Life, is against the war, and he refuses to allow his son to fight. However, Sam is determined to fight. He steals the family gun and runs off to join the Continental soldiers.

Tim is left to make a choice between his brother and his father. Tim has always looked up to his older brother with pride, but he is also convinced that his father must know something his brother is too young to understand. The boy becomes torn regarding his own ideas and loyalties. He supports Sam when the older boy says everyone should be free from British tyranny, but he also supports his father's belief that the colonists are already free.

As the story progresses, Tim must take on more responsibilities in his brother's absence, and the war comes closer to home. Tim journeys with his father to Verplancks Point to sell their cattle and to buy supplies for their tavern. It is irrelevant to Tim and his father whether they sell the cattle to the British or the Americans; they are simply in need of the money. While Tim's father does not support the war, he likewise does not do anything to sabotage the Patriot movement.

On their journey back home, Life is abducted by the Patriots as a traitor. Tim escapes and continues home with the needed supplies for his mother and the tavern, but he does not know what has become of his father. Tim and his mother hold out hope for his safe return, and they send for Sam to come home to help them run the tavern.

Tim's father dies of disease on a British prison ship in New York. It is never explained how Life got to a British prison; however, the reader must be struck with the irony of the times and circumstances that allow a Loyalist to die at British hands. After Life is abducted, Sam refuses to come home, and Tim is left to run the tavern with his mother.

Eventually, Sam returns home for a brief visit when his unit travels through Redding. Sam sneaks home one night to visit with his mother and brother, and while he is there, the three of them hear some of their cattle being stolen. Tim and Sam run to catch the thieves, but Tim stops to pen the remaining cattle while Sam follows the thieves (who happen to be his fellow soldiers).

When Sam catches them, the soldiers turn on him, declaring that Sam is the thief and that they had caught him butchering the cows. Sam is arrested for stealing his own cattle, and he is tried by the Patriot army and sentenced to death. Despite the attempts of Tim and his mother to correct this injustice, the story ends with the hanging of Sam Meeker by the Patriot army. The general has chosen to make an example of Sam, and since any leniency would show weakness on his part, the general carries out the wrongful execution.

Traditionally, history tells of the glorious revolutionary cause and the underdog's fight to victory. However, here is a seldom told story, based significantly in fact, that presents a fuller and more realistic picture of the conflict and tragedy behind the glory.

Vocabulary Lists

On this page are vocabulary lists that correspond to each sectional grouping of chapters. Vocabulary activity ideas can be found on page 9 in this book.

Section 1: Chapter 1–3

Patriots	agitators
Rebels	pride
Loyalists	lasciviousness
Lobsterbacks	bayonet
Tories	sin
rebellion	injustices
Parliament	envied
subversion	principles
treason	

Section 2: Chapter 4–6

Continentals	suspicious
disarm	pasture
deserter	petition
apprentice	surveyor
shilling	prison ships
dishonorable	

Section 3: Chapter 7–9

regiment	muskets
recalcitrance	raiders
pondering	livestock
almanac	gesturing
plundering	decency
colony	wharves
lawlessness	sturgeon
sedition	

Section 4: Chapter 10–12

fusillade	mortar
ammunition	forage
swaggering	flogged
enlistment	heifer
epidemic	mutiny
cholera	horizon
ideals	brute
pledge	badgering
unscrupulous	endure

Section 5: Chapter 13–Epilogue

adjunct	clemency
curt	stockade
shrugged	staggering
court-martial	

8

Vocabulary Activity Ideas

You can help your students learn and retain the vocabulary in *My Brother Sam Is Dead* by providing them with interesting vocabulary activities. Here are a few ideas to try.

❑ Many people of all ages like to make and solve puzzles. Ask your students to make their own **Crossword Puzzles** or **Word Search Puzzles** using the vocabulary words from the story.

❑ Challenge your students to a **Vocabulary Bee**. This is similar to a spelling bee, but in addition to spelling each word correctly, the game participants must correctly define the words as well.

❑ Play **Vocabulary Concentration**. The goal of this game is to match vocabulary words with their definitions. Divide the class into groups of two to five students. Have students make two sets of cards the same size and color. On one set have them write the vocabulary words. On the second set have them write the definitions. All cards are mixed together and placed facedown on a table. A player picks two cards. If the pair matches the word with its definition, the player keeps the cards and takes another turn. Players must concentrate to remember the locations of words and their definitions. The game continues until all matches have been made. This is an activity for free exploration time.

❑ Have your students practice their writing skills by creating sentences and paragraphs in which multiple vocabulary words are used correctly. Ask them to share their **Power Vocabulary** sentences and paragraphs with the class.

❑ Ask your students to write paragraphs which use the vocabulary words to present **History Lessons** that relate to the time period or historical events mentioned in the story.

❑ Challenge your students to use a specific vocabulary word from the story at least **Ten Times in One Day**. They must keep a record of when, how, and why the word was used.

❑ As a group activity, have students work together to create an **Illustrated Dictionary** of the vocabulary words.

❑ Play **Twenty Questions** with the entire class. In this game, one student selects a vocabulary word and gives clues about this word, one by one, until someone in the class can guess the word.

❑ Play **Vocabulary Charades**. In this game, vocabulary words are acted out.

❑ Have students **illustrate the vocabulary words** on one side of a sheet of paper. The word is written on the back. These can be used as a "quiz show" for a whole-class activity, with one student acting as moderator, or they can be placed on a bulletin board or hallway display with the words added at the bottom. As a variation, students may do impromptu drawings on the chalkboard, challenging classmates to guess the word.

You probably have many more ideas to add to this list. Try them! See if experiencing vocabulary on a personal level increases your students' vocabulary interest and retention.

Quiz Time

1. On the back of this paper, write a one-paragraph summary of the major events of the chapters in this section.

2. Why is Tim envious of his brother, Sam?

   _____

   _____

3. Why does Sam decide to join the Patriots?

   _____

   _____

4. Why does Sam say he cannot help milk Old Pru?

   _____

   _____

5. What does Sam want to take from his father and why?

   _____

   _____

6. Why does Sam's father kick him out of the house?

   _____

   _____

7. Why does Tom Warrups talk to Tim during church?

   _____

   _____

8. Who is Sam's girlfriend, and who is her father?

   _____

   _____

9. What do Sam and his girlfriend ask Tim to do at the tavern?

   _____

   _____

10. Who is returning to Redding at the end of Chapter 3?

    _____

    _____

Tim's Clothes

Glue Tim to a piece of construction paper and cut out the pattern. Use markers, colored pencils, or crayons to color the clothing. Cut out the clothing pieces and attach the clothes Tim would wear for an average day.

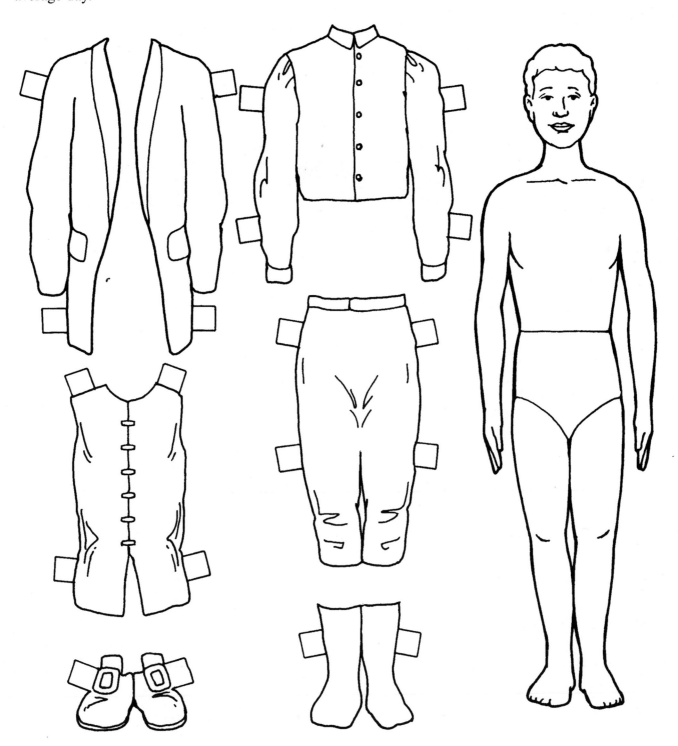

Extension: After you have helped dress Tim for the day, write a journal entry for him that tells what he did during that day.

Patriot or Tory?

Sam and Life Meeker disagree on which side to support in the war for independence. Sam believes that he needs to fight to be free, and Life believes that he already is free. Reread the first section of the book where Sam has just arrived home, and he and Life are debating the war.

Your job is to help Tim decide whether he should support the Patriots or the Tories. In groups of three, choose a side, find supporting quotes, and list reasons why they support your side. Present your reasons orally to the class. Be sure to cite supporting reasons from the book. Include at least two of your own ideas and opinions as well.

Patriot or Tory *(Circle one.)*

Citations from the Book

Page Number	Quote	Reason It Supports My Side

Personal Reasons

First

Second

Revolutionary War Time Line

In the opening scene of *My Brother Sam Is Dead*, Sam returns home to tell his family some news. The Patriot militia has had its first battle with the British army, and it was victorious. While this battle is technically the beginning of the military war between the Patriots and the British, it was not the start of the conflict. Many events that led up to the war occurred prior to the battle. Below are events that happened in the following years: 1765, 1772, 1773, 1775, 1776, 1779, and 1782. Cut out the events boxes and place them in chronological order on a time line. Use the sample time line as a guide.

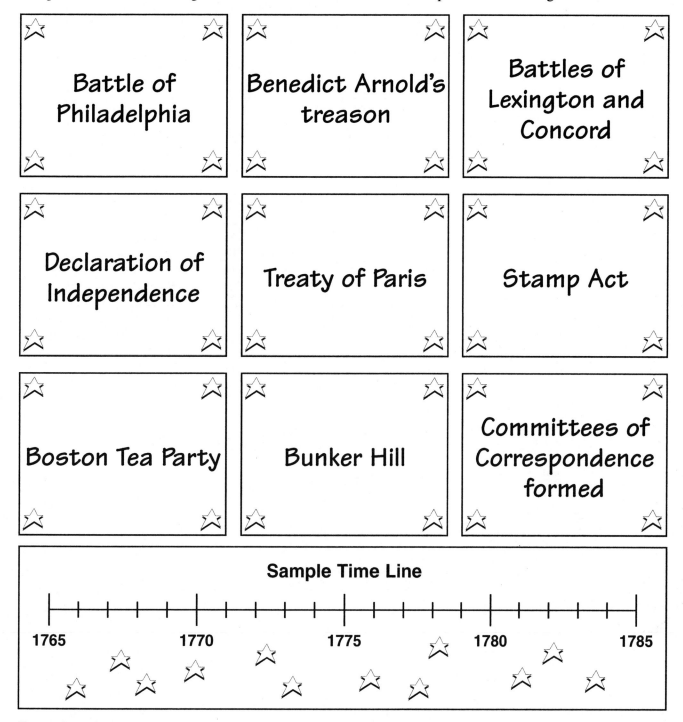

Battle of Philadelphia

Benedict Arnold's treason

Battles of Lexington and Concord

Declaration of Independence

Treaty of Paris

Stamp Act

Boston Tea Party

Bunker Hill

Committees of Correspondence formed

Sample Time Line

1765   1770   1775   1780   1785

Extension: Write a one-page report on one of the topics listed above.

My Brother or My Father?

Sam decides to join the Patriot movement against his father's wishes. Life is decidedly against the war and the Patriot cause. Tim is caught in the middle of their argument and is unable to decide which one he supports. He has always looked up to his brother because of his charisma and intelligence. Tim also respects his father's opinion because his father is older and knows more about everything. If you were Tim and had to make a decision based on your father's beliefs or your brother's, which would you choose?

First, answer the following questions:

Would you support your father or your brother? Why? _____

_____

_____

_____

_____

_____

_____

_____

Now, rank the following factors in order of importance for supporting either your father or brother and write why you ranked it as such.(1 = most important).

_____ trust _____

_____ intelligence _____

_____ common sense_____

_____ loyalty _____

_____ experience _____

_____ personal belief_____

_____ other _____

Get in a small group to talk about your decisions. Determine the beliefs you share and those about which you disagree. One member of the group will report your conclusions to the class.

Quiz Time

1. On the back of this paper, write a one-paragraph summary of the major events in the chapters of this section.

2. Why are the Continental soldiers looking for the Meeker family gun?

   _____

3. What does Tim think might happen to Father when the soldiers are in the tavern?

   _____

4. Why does Tim threaten to shoot Sam with the Brown Bess?

   _____

5. Why does Tim call Sam a coward? Do you think Sam is a coward? Explain.

   _____

   _____

6. What does Sam do when he sees his father?

   _____

7. In the beginning of Chapter 5, how does Tim describe the food supply in Redding?

   _____

   _____

8. Why is Life reluctant to let Tim work for Mr. Heron?

   _____

   _____

9. Why does Betsy Read try to steal Tim's letter?

   _____

   _____

10. What does the letter from Mr. Heron mean?

   _____

   _____

"Yankee Doodle Dandy"

While Tim is walking toward Mr. Heron's house to pick up the business letters, he is humming "Yankee Doodle Dandy." The tune of that song dates back to Holland in the 1500s. Over time, the song evolved with new lyrics. During the French and Indian Wars, an English army surgeon wrote the current lyrics to make fun of the untrained American soldiers. However, the Americans liked "Yankee Doodle Dandy" and adopted it as their own. The British hated the song by the end of the Revolutionary War because the Americans sang it so often. In fact, as the British were retreating from Yorktown, the Americans played "Yankee Doodle."

Yankee Doodle went to town,
Riding on a pony,
He stuck a feather in his cap
And called it macaroni.
Yankee Doodle keep it up,
Yankee Doodle dandy,
Mind the music and the step,
And with the girls be handy.

Using the music from "Yankee Doodle," write your own lyrics for the song. You can write your lyrics to make fun of the Americans or British or to support either side during the Revolutionary War.

My Lyrics

_____

_____

_____

_____

_____

_____

_____

Mr. Heron's Letters

Mr. Heron does not trust Tim to deliver the letter, so to test Tim he writes, "If this message is received, we will know that the messenger is reliable." As soon as Betsy and Tim open the letter, Tim is unable to deliver any more letters for Mr. Heron.

Pretend that Tim delivered the letter successfully and is on his second trip from Mr. Heron's home to see Mr. Burr. Your group's job is to write a second letter from Mr. Heron to Mr. Burr. If Tim had delivered the first letter, what do you think the second letter might have said, and how would it be addressed? After you have completed your letter, read it as a group to the class.

Dear _____,

_____

_____

_____

_____

_____

_____

_____

_____

_____

_____

_____

_____

Sincerely,

_____

Right to Bear Arms

Read and answer these questions.

1. In the fourth chapter of the book, Continental soldiers threaten to kill Tim's parents if they do not hand over their gun. Why do you think the soldiers want the Meeker's gun?

   _____

   _____

   _____

   _____

2. After the war, when the founders of the United States were writing the Constitution and the Bill of Rights, they included the Second Amendment. The Second Amendment states ". . . the right of the people to keep and bear arms shall not be infringed." Why do you think the founders included this in the Bill of Rights?

   _____

   _____

   _____

   _____

3. Debate over the Second Amendment has continued into today's society. Many people have different interpretations of this amendment, and some think the amendment should be taken out of the Bill of Rights. What do you think?

   _____

   _____

   _____

   _____

4. Find a newspaper article that discusses the right to bear arms. Summarize it here.

   _____

   _____

   _____

   _____

Lying to Your Parents

Read the paragraph and answer the questions that follow.

Mr. Heron comes to visit the tavern and asks Life to let Tim work for him. Life does not like the idea of Tim carrying letters for Mr. Heron, and he will not allow Tim to do so. Tim decides to disobey his father and to work for Mr. Heron secretly.

1. How does Tim justify disobeying his father?

_____

_____

_____

_____

2. Have you ever disobeyed your parents for a reason you thought was justified? What did you do, and what was your justification?

_____

_____

_____

_____

3. Did your parents or someone else catch you?

_____

_____

_____

_____

4. Was the activity worth the punishment you incurred or might have incurred?

_____

_____

_____

_____

Quiz Time

1. On the back of this paper, write a one-paragraph summary of the major events from the chapters of this section.

2. Why does Tim's father object to his mother writing a letter to Sam? _____

   _____

   _____

3. Why does Tim's father ask Tim to go to Verplancks Point with him? _____

   _____

4. Why do the cow-boys harass Tim and his father?_____

   _____

   _____

   _____

5. Who are the people who scare off the cow-boys, and why are they willing to help Tim and his father?

   _____

   _____

6. Who are the Platts? _____

   _____

7. What does Tim think about life at Verplancks Point?_____

   _____

   _____

8. Why do Tim and his father decide to return through Ridgebury on their way home?_____

   _____

9. What does Tim do when he thinks his father has been gone too long? _____

   _____

10. How does Tim get the cow-boys to leave him alone so he can travel home safely? _____

   _____

Packing for a Journey

Imagine that Tim and his father are setting out for a journey to Verplancks Point. They must pack everything they will need for the entire journey. Pretend that you are going on this trip with them. What types of things would you take and why? (An example has been done for you.)

Note: Remember that during the Revolutionary War people did not have all the things we have today. Choose items that were available during the period of the book.

Item	Types	Why
food	beef jerky, bread	They can be kept easily, and I will not need to cook.

Extension: Bring in at least one item from your chart to share with the class. Explain your item to the class and why you think you will need it on the trip to Verplancks Point.

Traveling to Verplancks Point

The dashed line on the map below charts Life and Tim's journey to Verplancks Point. Label the map using the places listed in the boxes below. Describe and illustrate a major event that occurred at each of the places marked by an asterisk (*).

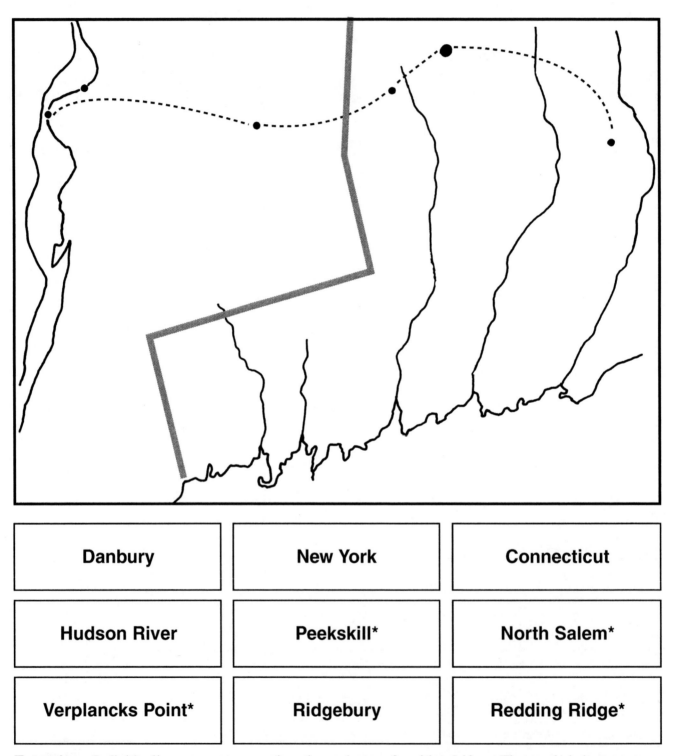

Danbury	**New York**	**Connecticut**
Hudson River	**Peekskill***	**North Salem***
Verplancks Point*	**Ridgebury**	**Redding Ridge***

Extension: Individually or as a group, write a journal entry for either Life or Tim on their journey to Verplancks Point.

War Supplies

During war, societies often need to ration materials and goods to help support the military. In the book, Tim states that supplies are short during the Revolutionary War. Give reasons why you think the following supplies are in short supply.

food _____

_____

guns/ammunition _____

_____

cloth _____

_____

leather _____

_____

farming tools _____

_____

construction materials _____

_____

Interview someone who has lived through and remembers a war such as World War II or Vietnam. Ask if he or she can remember any supplies that were limited or difficult to obtain. Find out which supplies were hard to find and why. (You will need to write about at least four.)

Person Interviewed: _____

Supply   **Reason**

1. _____   _____

                                          _____

2. _____   _____

                                          _____

3. _____   _____

                                          _____

4. _____   _____

                                          _____

Sinfulness

Throughout the novel Tim is worried about committing a sin. When Tim disobeys his parents, he is more concerned about committing a sin than he is about his parents catching him. List some of the things Tim does that he feels are sinful and describe why he feels this way. Also include whether you agree or disagree with Tim. An example has been done for you.

Act	Sin	What I Think
visiting Sam at Tom Warrups' home	lying	I disagree with Tim because it is all right to lie for a good reason. (or) I agree with Tim because lying to your parents is wrong no matter what.

Quiz Time

1. On the back of this paper, write a one-paragraph summary of the major events from the chapters of this section.

2. What happens to the prices in the tavern?_____

_____

3. Why does Mother think Sam will come home if he knows his father has been taken prisoner?

_____

_____

4. What changes happen in Tim when he gets the wagon home by himself?

_____

_____

5. Why do the English soldiers take Captain Betts, Mr. Rogers, and Jerry Sanford?

_____

_____

6. What happens to Ned?_____

_____

_____

7. Why does Mother refuse to let Tim help Captain Betts? _____

_____

8. Why is Sam afraid to go home to visit Tim and Mother?_____

_____

_____

9. How does Father die? _____

_____

10. Why do the cattle thieves accuse Sam of being the thief? _____

_____

Revolutionary War Flags

In Chapter 10 Tim watches the British troops arrive in Redding. His first glimpse of the mighty army is the vanguard. The vanguard displays the flags of the army, and a drummer boy announces their arrival. In the next chapter, Sam and the Patriot army occupy the city of Redding. When they set up camp, they display their flags.

Continental Colors

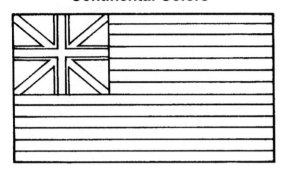

St. George's Cross

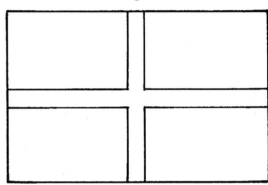

British Union Jack

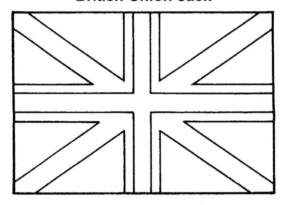

The British used two flags during the American Revolution. England's St. George's Cross represented England and had been used by the English for over 700 years. This flag flew beside the British Union Jack, which represented the entire British Empire. The Union Jack was not officially adopted until after the Revolutionary War, but it was widely used before its official adoption.

The colonies were forming a new country, and in 1775 they adopted the Continental colors to represent their cause. Americans chose 13 stripes to represent the 13 colonies. The Union Jack was added to the original flag to show that the colonists did not originally seek full independence. They were willing to cooperate with England, but England did not want to cooperate with the colonists. This flag became the national flag until the Stars and Stripes were adopted in 1777.

Now, it is your turn to create a flag to represent yourself, class, school, or town. Be careful in choosing colors and symbols for your flag. You can use all types of media to create your flag, including markers, colored pencils, computer images, construction paper, tissue paper, yarn, and so forth. Be creative! Either on the back of the flag or on a separate sheet of paper, write the meaning of your flag and explain why you chose your colors and symbols.

What Now, Sam?

At the end of Chapter 12, the soldiers who steal the cows arrest Sam as the thief. Why do they do this?

_____

_____

Divide into small groups. Discuss what you think will happen next. Write everyone's ideas here.

Now, take a vote on what the group as a whole thinks will most likely happen next. Write it here.

_____

As a class, share each group's findings. Have a secretary write down everything and keep your ideas until the end of the book to see how closely you predicted.

Crispus Attucks

At the end of Chapter 10, Tim witnesses the killing of the Rebels, including the slave, Ned. Ned is a slave, but he still fights for the Americans who enslave him. Ned is not the only black man to give his life for the American cause of freedom.

On March 15, 1770, a runaway slave named Crispus Attucks appeared on the streets of Boston to lead America toward revolution. A white mob was approaching the Customs House in Boston to protest the newly arrived British troops. The angry mob was without a leader until Attucks appeared from the crowd, calling the mob forward by yelling, "We're not afraid of them! Knock 'em over. They dare not fire."

The black leader formed his group of white men in Dock Square and led them to attack the Customs House. As he reached the soldiers, they fired, and Attucks was one of the first to fall. History would record the day as the Boston Massacre.

Three years later John Adams wrote a letter from "Crispus Attucks" to Governor Hutchinson of Massachusetts. This letter placed the blame for his death on the British and asked why he was killed.

Sir,

You will hear from Us with Astonishment. You ought to hear from Us with Horror. You are chargeable before God and Man, with our Blood. —The Soldiers were but passive instruments . . . in our Destruction . . . You were a free Agent. You acted coolly, deliberately, with . . . Malice, not against Us in Particular but against the People in general, which in the Sight of the law is . . . Murder. You will hear from Us hereafter.

Crispus Attucks

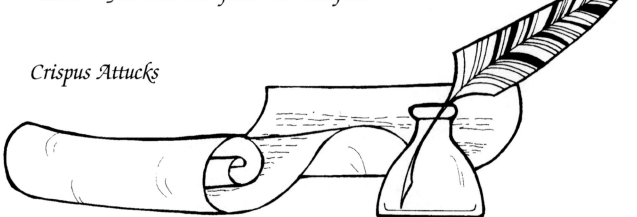

Now you will write a letter. Address it to the British soldiers who killed Ned. Write the letter as if it were written by Ned himself, asking questions that he might have had about his death. Use John Adams' letter as a model.

Help Us, General Parsons

Pretend that you are Tim. If you saw your brother being arrested for cattle thievery, what would you write in a letter to General Parsons to convince him to release Sam? Write a letter to General Parsons explaining Sam's innocence. Present your reasons clearly.

Dear General Parsons,

Sincerely,
Tim Meeker

Extension: Give your letter to an impartial reader. Have the reader decide whether Sam should be freed based on the evidence in the letter.

Quiz Time

1. On the back of this paper, write a one-paragraph summary of the major events from the chapters in this section.

2. What happens when Tim originally goes to see Colonel Parsons after Sam is arrested?

   _____

   _____

3. What do Tim and his mother do before they go to cut the beef from the cow?

   _____

4. Why does Colonel Parsons think that General Putnam will not allow Sam to be pardoned?

   _____

   _____

5. What does Colonel Read believe will happen to Sam?

   _____

   _____

   _____

6. Describe Sam's attitude after he finds out he will be shot as a cattle thief.

   _____

7. Describe Mother's attitude after she learns Sam will be executed.

   _____

8. Describe Tim's plan to break Sam from prison.

   _____

9. Why does Tim feel he needs to attend the execution?

   _____

10. In the epilogue, what reason or reasons does Tim give for writing this story?

   _____

   _____

Battles of the War

Place the letters of these famous battles on the map to show their locations during the Revolutionary War.

a. Bunker Hill

b. Lexington and Concord

c. Yorktown

d. Trenton

e. Saratoga

f. Princeton

g. Fort Ticonderoga

h. Monmouth

i. Guilford Court House

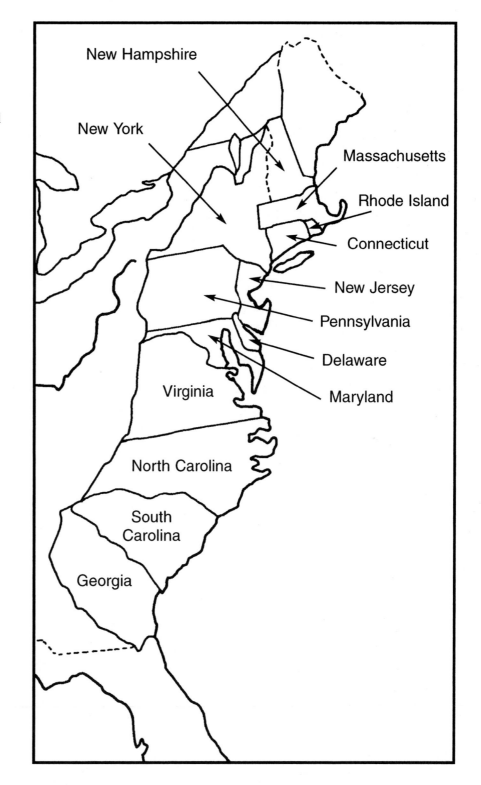

Note: Keep this map handy for the culminating project.

Internet Scavenger Hunt

Use the Internet for Revolutionary War research. Look to this Web site: *The Revolutionary War: A Journey Towards Freedom.* At the site, you can read about famous historical figures of the Revolutionary War and answer the questions below.

Step 1:　Type in http://library.advanced.org/10966/ to go to the site.

Step 2:　Click on the Infopedia Star at the left of the screen.

Step 3:　Click on Historical Figures Collection.

Step 4:　Choose a historical figure on whom to report.

Name: _____

Birthplace and date: _____

What was your historical figure's occupation before the Revolutionary War? _____

_____

Why did this person join the Revolutionary War effort? _____

_____

_____

What are your famous person's significant involvements during the war? _____

_____

_____

What did this famous person do after the war? _____

_____

_____

Additional notes:_____

_____

_____

After you have completed your research, you will need to adopt the personality of the character to give a presentation to the class, explaining your (the character's) life and why you were involved in the Revolutionary War. In your presentation be sure to report and act as if you were the figure during the time of the war.

Extension: If you have extra time, explore the site for more exciting information about the Revolutionary War. Tell the class what you found.

Casualty Graph

In every battle of the Revolutionary War, people were injured and killed on both sides. Choose a Revolutionary War battle and show the number of casualties from each side on the bar graph on page 34. Once you have completed the graph, answer the following questions.

Battle: _____

1. Find the percentages of soldiers killed and wounded in your chosen battle.

    Percentage of Patriots killed _____

    Percentage of Patriots wounded_____

    Percentage of British killed _____

    Percentage of British wounded _____

2. Based on the percentages, which side do you think won the battle? Why? _____

    _____

    _____

    _____

    _____

    _____

    _____

3. Which side had more wounded soldiers? _____

4. Which side had more soldiers killed? _____

5. Find out which side is considered to have won the battle. Does it match your prediction based on the percentages? Why or why not?

    _____

    _____

    _____

    _____

    _____

Casualty Graph *(cont.)*

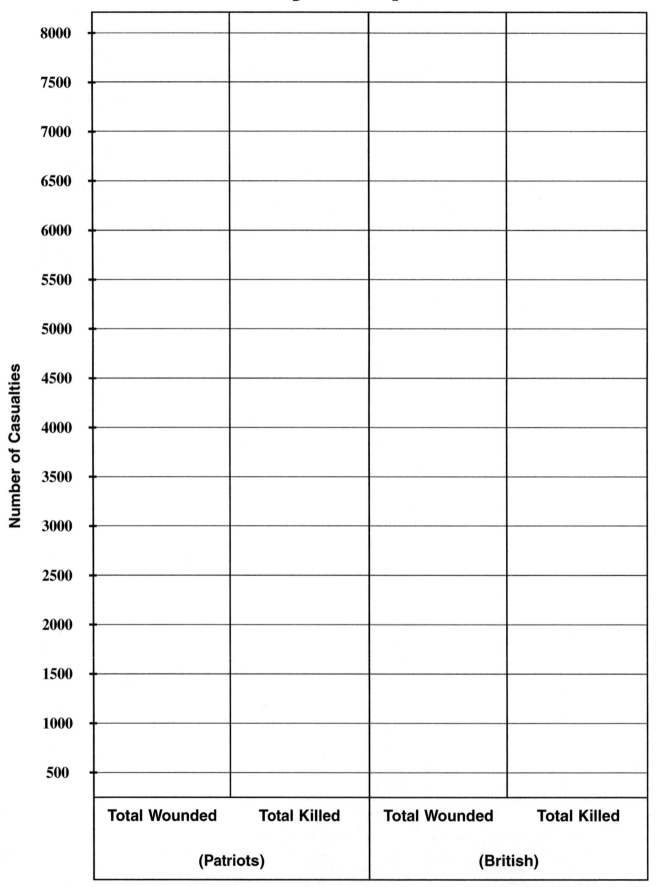

Sam's Eulogy

Write a eulogy commemorating the life of Sam Meeker. Be sure to write about his accomplishments, his personality, his unjust execution, and how he will be remembered in the future.

Extension: Read your eulogy for Sam to the class or in a small group.

Book Report Ideas

There are numerous ways to report on a book. After you have finished reading *My Brother Sam Is Dead*, choose one method of reporting that interests you. It may be a way that your teacher suggests, an idea of your own, or one of the ways listed below.

- **See What I Read?**
  This report is a visual one. A model of a scene from the story can be created, or a likeness of one or more of the characters from the story can be drawn or sculpted.

- **Time Capsule**
  This report provides people living at a future time with the reasons why *My Brother Sam Is Dead* is such an outstanding book, and it gives these future people reasons why the book should be read. Make a time capsule-type design and neatly print or write your reasons inside the capsule. You may wish to hide your capsule after you have shared it with your classmates. Perhaps one day someone will find it and read *My Brother Sam Is Dead* because of what you wrote!

- **Come to Life**
  This report is one that lends itself to a group project. A size-appropriate group prepares a scene from the story for dramatization, acts it out, and relates the significance of the scene to the entire book. Costumes and props will add to the dramatization.

- **Letter to the Author**
  In this report, you can write a letter to Christopher Collier or James Lincoln Collier. Tell the author what you liked about *My Brother Sam Is Dead* and ask him any questions you may have about the writing of the book. You may even want to give him some suggestions for a sequel. After your teacher has read it and you have made your writing the best it can be, send it to him in care of the publishing company.

- **Guess Who or What**
  This report takes the form of several games of "Twenty Questions." The reporter gives a series of clues about a character from the story in a vague-to-precise or general-to-specific order. After all clues have been given, the identity of the mystery character must be deduced. After the character has been guessed, the same reporter presents another "Twenty Questions" about an event in the story.

- **In Today's World**
  Suppose one of the characters in *My Brother Sam Is Dead* came to life and walked into your home or classroom. This report gives a view of what this character sees, hears, and feels as he or she experiences the world in which you live.

- **Sales Talk**
  This report serves as an advertisement to "sell" *My Brother Sam Is Dead* to one or more specific groups. You decide on the group to target and the sales pitch you will use. Create a magazine advertisement to use in your presentation.

- **Coming Attraction**
  My Brother Sam Is Dead is about to be made into a movie, and you have been chosen to design the promotional poster. Include the title and author of the book, a listing of the main characters and the contemporary actors who will play them, a drawing of a scene from the book, and a paragraph synopsis of the story.

Research Ideas

Describe three things you read in *My Brother Sam Is Dead* that you want to learn more about.

1. _____

2. _____

3. _____

As you read *My Brother Sam Is Dead,* you encountered geographical locations, important groups at the time of the war, historical events, and historical characters. To understand the story better, research to find out more about these people, places, and things.

Work in groups to research one or more of the areas you named above or the areas that are mentioned below. Share your findings with the rest of the class in any appropriate form of oral presentation.

Groups

- Minutemen
- Anglican Church
- Continental Army
- Loyalists
- Patriots
- Constitutional Congress
- Connecticut General Assembly

Historical Events/Locations

- Battles of Lexington and Concord
- Boston Tea Party
- Bunker Hill
- Fort Ticonderoga
- Battle of New York
- Valley Forge
- Redding, Connecticut

Historical Characters

- John Adams
- John Hancock
- Captain Benedict Arnold
- King George III
- Edmund Burke
- George Washington
- Aaron Burr

Famous Battles in the News

In *My Brother Sam Is Dead*, it was difficult for Tim to decide which side to support because every event changed his mind. All the events that occurred during the war were subject to interpretation by the people who wrote about them. For example, when Sam wrote home about the Battle of New York, he wrote like it was a great Patriot victory, but the British had really won the battle.

Your job is to write a newspaper article on a battle from the Revolutionary War. You will write your article from the perspective of a Patriot or a Loyalist. The Loyalists of the time wrote for the *Rivington Gazette,* and the Patriots wrote for the *Connecticut Journal*. Newspaper reporters for the *Rivington Gazette* would almost always make the British look victorious, and the *Connecticut Journal* would almost always make the Patriots the victorious ones.

Follow these directions.

1. Choose a battle or event from the items listed below.

2. Decide whether you are going to represent the British or the Patriots and write for the appropriate newspaper.

3. Do some research on the battle or event to find out the true facts. Use the form on page 39. Remember that you will need to use these facts to support your side's position.

4. Write a rough draft of a newspaper article on a regular sheet of paper.

5. After you have read the article and it has been corrected, rewrite the article onto the appropriate newspaper form (page 40 or 41).

6. Draw an illustration or political cartoon to accompany the article.

Battles and Events

- Boston Tea Party
- Boston Massacre
- Brandywine
- Bunker Hill
- Camden
- Freeman's Farm (first battle)
- Freeman's Farm (second battle)
- Germantown

- Battles of Lexington and Concord
- Long Island
- Monmouth
- Princeton
- Trenton
- Yorktown
- Declaration of Independence
- Kings Mountain

Famous Battles in the News *(cont.)*

Event name: _____

Date of the event: _____

Location of the event: _____

Number of Americans involved: _____

    killed/wounded: _____

Number of British involved: _____

    killed/wounded: _____

Give a summary of the battle or event. _____

_____

_____

_____

_____

_____

List any important historical figure involved or present at the event/battle. Tell how the historical figure was involved.

_____

_____

_____

_____

_____

List any important events that proceeded or caused the battle/event.

_____

_____

_____

_____

Famous Battles in the News *(cont.)*

Rivington Gazette

Famous Battles in the News *(cont.)*

Connecticut Journal

Unit Test

Matching: Match the characters with their descriptions.

_____ 1. Mr. Heron   a. against the war

_____ 2. Sam   b. torn between both sides of the war

_____ 3. Betsy Read   c. Patriot soldier

_____ 4. Tim   d. Native American friend

_____ 5. Life Meeker   e. Sam's girlfriend

_____ 6. Tom Warrups   f. neighbor who helps both the English and the Patriots

True or False: Write true or false next to each statement.

_____ 1. Colonel Benedict Arnold leads the English army.

_____ 2. Colonel Parsons wants to help Tim get Sam out of jail.

_____ 3. Life Meeker is excited to travel to Verplancks Point.

_____ 4. Tim wants to become a surveying apprentice for Mr. Heron immediately.

_____ 5. Tim threatens to shoot Sam.

_____ 6. Sam runs away to join the Patriot army.

_____ 7. The English army kills Sam.

_____ 8. Betsy Read is a Tory.

_____ 9. Cow-boys kidnap Life Meeker.

_____ 10. Sam is arrested for being a cattle thief.

Short Answer: Answer these questions in complete sentences.

1. In which state does the Meeker family live? _____

2. What family do Tim and his father stay with on their way to Verplancks Point?

   _____

3. Who is the Patriot army leader in Redding? _____

4. In what major battle does Sam fight, and what does he say about it in his letter home?

   _____

5. What happens to Jerry Sanford? _____

Essay: Respond to the following in detail on the back of this paper.

1. Describe why Life Meeker is against the war.

2. Explain why Tim has a difficult time deciding whether to be a Patriot or a Loyalist. Give examples of times when he says that he favors each side.

Response Test

Explain the meaning and significance of each of these quotations from *My Brother Sam Is Dead*.

Chapter 1   *". . . idle hands make the Devil's work."* (Mother)

Chapter 2   *"Render therefore unto Caesar the things which are Caesar's."* (Rev. Beach)

Chapter 3   *"That's subversion and we don't permit subversion here."* (Father)

Chapter 4   *"We know you have one. We know where all the Tory weapons in Redding are. Not everybody is willing to play dog to the King."* (Continental Soldier)

                   "Don't come any closer, Sam, or I'll shoot you." (Tim)

Chapter 6   *"If this message is received, we know that the messenger is reliable."* (Mr. Heron)

Chapter 7   *"Times have changed, Meeker. Now we want to know who's doing the eating. And we don't want to be Lobsterbacks. There's only one place where beef goes from Verplancks Point and that's New York. And the British army owns New York."* (cow-boy)

Chapter 8   *"If wishes were horses beggars would ride."* (Father)

Chapter 9   *"Father said that the escort would be along soon, but when you didn't come I was worried that the cow-boys would get to me first."* (Tim)

Chapter 11   *"But we were expecting some Continental troops. You've heard of General Benedict Arnold, I expect?"* (wounded Continental soldier)

                   " 'Oh, Lord,' she said, 'Please take this war away from here. What have we done to endure this? Why must it go on so long? What have we done in Thy sight to deserve this evil?' " (Mother)

Chapter 12   *"In war the dead pay the debts for the living."* (Father)

                   "And now I go to enjoy the freedom war has brought me." (Father)

                   "A short life but a merry one." (Continental soldier)

                   " 'Timmy, get Colonel Parsons,' he cried. 'They're taking me in as a cattle thief.' " (Sam)

Chapter 14   *"Let the dead bury the dead."* (Mother)

                   "Going to get yourself killed, son?" (Mother)

Teacher Note: Choose an appropriate number of quotes for your students.

Conversations

Work in size-appropriate groups to write and perform the conversations that might have occurred in each of the following situations.

- Reverend Beach tries to convince Sam to stay home instead of fighting for the Patriots. (*2 people*)

- Sam, Colonel Parsons, and General Putnam talk before Sam's execution. (*3 people*)

- Father (if he had lived) and General Putnam talk before Sam's execution. (*2 people*)

- Tim and Jerry Sanford talk while Jerry is on the prison ship. (*2 people*)

- Sam and Betsy Read meet while Sam is in prison awaiting his execution. (*2 people*)

- Tim and Tom Warrups discuss Sam joining the Patriot army. (*2 people*)

- Sam and the Patriots who arrested Life discuss the justice of arresting him. (*3 people*)

- Life and Colonel Read talk about the reasons for fighting the war. (*2 people*)

- Tim and a boy his age who works on the river at Verplancks Point talk about their lifestyles. (*2 people*)

- Sam and Betsy Read talk just before Sam leaves to join the Patriot army. (*2 people*)

- Colonel Read and General Putnam discuss whether or not Sam should be released. (*2 people*)

- Mother and Sam meet before Sam is executed. (*2 people*)

- Mother and the cow-boys who kidnapped Life meet face to face. (*3–4 people*)

Bibliography of Related Reading

Avi. ***The Fighting Ground***. J. P. Lippincott, 1984.

Brenner, Barbara. ***If You Were There in 1776.*** Bradbury Press, 1994.

Collier, Christopher and James Lincoln. ***The Bloody Country***. Scholastic, 1976.

    The Winter Hero. Four Winds Press, 1978.

Davis, Burke. ***Black Heroes of the American Revolution.*** Harcourt Brace, 1976.

Forbes, Esther. ***Johnny Tremain.*** Houghton Mifflin, 1971.

Fritz, Jean. ***Can't You Make Them Behave, King George?*** Putnam & Grossett Group, 1977.

    Traitor: The Case of Benedict Arnold. Putnam & Grossett Group, 1981.

    Where Was Patrick Henry on the 29th of May? Coward, McCann & Geoghegan, Inc., 1975.

Moore, Kay. ***If You Lived at the Time of the American Revolution.*** Scholastic, 1997.

Penner, Lucille Recht. ***The Liberty Tree: The Beginning of the American Revolution.*** Random House, 1998.

Young, Robert. ***The Real Patriots of the American Revolution.*** Dillon Press, 1997.

Zeinert, Karen. ***The Remarkable Women of the American Revolution.*** Millbrook Press, 1996.

Relate Books from Teacher Created Materials

TCM 293—*Revolutionary War* (Thematic Unit)

TCM 440—*Johnny Tremain* (Literature Unit)

TCM 480—*American History* Simulations

TCM 587—*Colonial America* (Thematic Unit)

TCM 2203—*Technology Connections for Colonial America*

Answer Key

Page 10

1. Answers will vary.
2. Tim is envious of Sam because he seems so intelligent and speaks in an interesting and quick-witted way.
3. Sam decides to join the Patriots because he wants to be free and because his friends are joining the cause.
4. Sam says he cannot help to milk Old Pru because he does not have any old clothes, and he does not want to dirty his new uniform.
5. Sam wants to take the Brown Bess (gun) to use in the war. If he does not take it, he will be a soldier without a gun.
6. Life kicks Sam out of the house because he does not approve of Sam fighting in the war, and he does not want him to take the family gun.
7. Tom Warrups talks to Tim during church because he wants Tim to know that Sam is staying at his house.
8. Sam's girlfriend is Betsy Read, and her father is Colonel Read, one of the leaders of the Patriot army.
9. Sam and Betsy ask Tim to listen to people in the tavern so he can find out who favors which side of the war.
10. Sam is returning to Redding.

Page 13

Stamp Act—1765

Committees of Correspondence formed—1772

Boston Tea Party—1773

Battles of Lexington and Concord—April 19, 1775

Bunker Hill—June 12, 1775

Declaration of Independence—1776

Battle of Philadelphia—1777

Benedict Arnold's treason—1780

Treaty of Paris—1782

Page 15

1. Answers will vary.

2. The Continental soldiers are taking all the guns from people they believe are still loyal to the British, and they believe the Meekers are such Loyalists.
3. Tim thinks the soldiers might kill his mother and father because they do not have the gun.
4. Tim threatens to shoot Sam because he is afraid that if he does not bring the gun to the house, the soldiers will kill his parents, and Sam isn't willing to give Tim the gun.
5. Tim calls Sam a coward because he will not face his parents or the soldiers at the tavern. Accept all appropriate responses to the second part of the question.
6. Sam waves and runs away.
7. Tim says that food and supplies are hard to find and very expensive because of the war.
8. Life will not let Tim work for Mr. Heron because he believes that Mr. Heron will put Tim in danger. Life does not believe Mr. Heron wants Tim simply to carry business letters.
9. Betsy Read tries to steal Tim's letter because she is afraid that there is information in the letter about where the Patriot soldiers are located, and she does not want Sam to get hurt.
10. Mr. Heron is testing Tim to see if he will really deliver the message. Mr. Heron does not write anything important in case Tim does not deliver the message.

Page 20

1. Answers will vary.
2. Life does not want Tim's mother to write to Sam because he does not want to encourage Sam to continue to fight with the Patriots.
3. Tim's father asks Tim to go to Verplancks Point because there is nobody else who can go with him, and he cannot travel there with the cattle on his own.
4. The cow-boys harass Tim and Life because they want to take the cattle for themselves and be sure they are not sold to British soldiers.

Answer Key *(cont.)*

5. The people who scare off the cow-boys are local citizens who ride around to keep the roads safe. They are willing to help Tim and his father because they are Loyalists and they believe Tim and Life are too.

6. The Platts are cousins of the Meekers. Life stays with them every year on his way to Verplancks Point.

7. Tim finds Verplancks Point fascinating at first because of the river, but after awhile he is happy to return to Redding.

8. Tim and Life decide to go back through Ridgebury because it is starting to snow, and it is the shortest route home.

9. Tim runs ahead and leaves the wagon behind to see if he can find his father.

10. Tim pretends that the cow-boys are really the escort he was hoping for. He tricks the cow-boys into believing that the escort will arrive soon.

Page 22

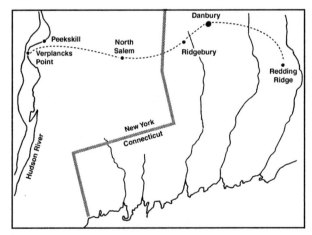

Redding Ridge: Tim lives near here and has to pass through the ridge to begin his journey to Verplancks Point.

North Salem: The Platt family lives here, and the Meekers stay here with the Platts

Peekskll: Tim's first and last look at the Hudson River is from here.

Verplancks Point: Tim and his father come here to sell their cattle. It is a river town with a great deal of trading and fishing.

Page 23

Answers will vary. However, here are some ideas that may be included.

food: Most of the food must go to the soldiers, and there are not many men at home to help grow more food.

guns/ammunition: All the guns and ammunition are either confiscated by the military or in use by the military in some way. There is not any place to buy extra guns, so the Americans must use all the guns the families already have.

cloth: The cloth is needed to clothe the soldiers and to make their uniforms.

leather: Leather is needed for the soldiers. They use leather for their belts and other supplies they carry.

farming tools: There is no one to make farming tools. Almost all the available men are either soldiers or employed to help the soldiers, and people are not available to make the necessary farming tools.

construction materials: As the soldiers progress across the colonies, they need to build housing, roads, and headquarters. All construction materials are needed for these purposes.

Page 25

1. Answers will vary.

2. The prices in the tavern continue to rise because of inflation and lack of supplies.

3. Mother thinks that Sam will see how much he is needed at home and then come home to help take care of his family since Father has been taken.

4. Tim finds himself to be very responsible and willing to work and help his Mother after he gets the wagon home by himself. Tim feels that he needs to take on some of his father's responsibilities because his father is not there.

5. The English take them as prisoners because they are Patriot leaders.

6. British soldiers kill Ned while he is defending a small house with other Patriots.

Answer Key *(cont.)*

7. Mother feels that she has already lost one son and her husband to the war, and she is not going to let Tim get involved at all.

8. Sam does not want to go home and visit Tim and his Mother because he is afraid that they will be angry with him and blame him for his father's abduction.

9. Life dies of cholera on a British prison ship.

10. The cattle thieves take Sam in as a cattle thief because if they did not, they would be hanged for the crime. There are two of them, and together they can deny culpability.

Page 30

1. Answers will vary.

2. Colonel Parsons is asleep, and the soldier will not wake him to help Sam.

3. Tim and his mother pray for Sam and the end of the war.

4. Colonel Parsons thinks that General Putnam wants an example to be made of soldiers who steal cattle, and he wants to kill Sam to keep the support of the local citizens. General Putnam does not care if Sam is guilty or innocent.

5. Colonel Read thinks that Sam is going to be executed.

6. Sam seems calm and a little bit hopeful that Tim might be able to help him.

7. Mother acts as if nothing is going to happen to Sam. She is very calm and tired.

8. Tim is going to run down to the prison and throw over a bayonet to Sam so that he can break out.

9. Tim feels that Sam would want him at the execution so that he will not be alone.

10. Tim is writing this story in order to memorialize Sam's short life and to show people who did not live through the war that although the outcome of the war made the country prosperous, many people who were relatively free before the war lost their lives to give others freedom.

Page 31

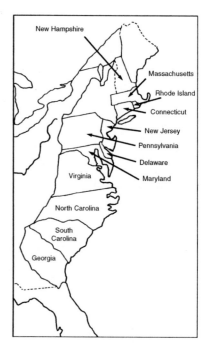

Page 42
Matching

1. f	3. e	5. a
2. c	4. b	6. d

True on False

1. false	4. false	7. false	10. true
2. true	5. true	8. false	
3. false	6. true	9. true	

Short Answer

1. The Meeker family lives in Connecticut.

2. Tim and Life stay with the Platt family on their way to Verplancks Point.

3. Colonel Read is the Patriot leader in Redding.

4. Sam fights in the battle of Long Island (New York) and writes home as if it is a Patriot victory.

5. Jerry Sanford is taken prisoner by the British and dies on a British prison ship.

Essay

Responses will vary. Be sure that whatever is written, it is well supported.